7521 3586

W9-AVM-315

STEM
SUPERSTAR
WOMEN

KATHERINE
JOHNSON

Guiding Spacecraft

Megan Borgert-Spaniol

Checkerboard
Library

An Imprint of Abdo Publishing
abdopublishing.com

abdopublishing.com

Published by Abdo Publishing, a division of ABDO, PO Box 398166, Minneapolis, Minnesota 55439. Copyright © 2018 by Abdo Consulting Group, Inc. International copyrights reserved in all countries. No part of this book may be reproduced in any form without written permission from the publisher. Checkerboard Library™ is a trademark and logo of Abdo Publishing.

Printed in the United States of America, North Mankato, Minnesota
102017
012018

THIS BOOK CONTAINS
RECYCLED MATERIALS

Design: Emily O'Malley, Mighty Media, Inc.
Production: Mighty Media, Inc.
Editor: Liz Salzmann
Cover Photograph: NASA
Interior Photographs: AP Images, p. 20; Bill Ingalls/NASA, p. 27; David C. Brown/NASA, p. 5; NASA, pp. 9, 15, 19; NASA Langley Research Center, p. 13; U.S. Air Force, p. 17; West Virginia and Regional History Collection, West Virginia University Libraries, pp. 7, 28 (right); Wikimedia Commons, pp. 11, 23, 25, 28 (left), 29 (left and right)

Publisher's Cataloging-in-Publication Data
Names: Borgert-Spaniol, Megan, author.
Title: Katherine Johnson: guiding spacecraft / by Megan Borgert-Spaniol.
Other titles: Guiding spacecraft
Description: Minneapolis, Minnesota : Abdo Publishing, 2018. | Series: STEM superstar women | Includes online resources and index.
Identifiers: LCCN 2017944050 | ISBN 9781532112812 (lib.bdg.) | ISBN 9781532150531 (ebook)
Subjects: LCSH: Johnson, Katherine G., 1918-.--Juvenile literature. | African American women mathematicians--Juvenile literature. | Mathematicians--United States--Biography--Juvenile literature.
Classification: DDC 510.92 [B]--dc23
LC record available at https://lccn.loc.gov/2017944050

CONTENTS

1

KATHERINE JOHNSON

Katherine Johnson began her professional career as an elementary school and high school teacher in Virginia. When she retired about 50 years later, she was the mathematician who sent the first Americans into space. Johnson helped break scientific **barriers** to space exploration. She also broke racial and gender barriers.

Johnson's career took off when much of America was still **segregated** by race. It was also a time when professional women were granted lower status than their male coworkers. As an African-American woman, Johnson experienced the race and gender **discrimination** of her time. But she refused to let it influence her opportunities.

> **"If you lose your curiosity, then you stop learning."**
>
> –Katherine Johnson

Johnson was instrumental in both space travel calculations and research. In her career, she wrote 26 scientific papers!

Johnson gave others her respect, and she expected the same in return.

Now in her late nineties, Johnson is modest about her achievements. She credits her success to her love of learning. A natural teacher, Johnson continues to inspire learners of all ages to ask questions and stay curious.

2

READY FOR THE FAST TRACK

Katherine Coleman was born on August 26, 1918, in White Sulphur Springs, West Virginia. She was the youngest of four children born to Joylette and Joshua Coleman. Katherine's mother was a former teacher. Her father was a farmer.

Katherine has said that she was born liking math. From an early age, she thought in numbers. She would count steps as she walked to church. She counted plates as she washed dishes. Young Katherine was so eager to start learning that she would follow her older brother to school.

When Katherine could finally start school herself, she was already advanced. She skipped first grade and went straight to second. A few years later, Katherine leapt from fourth to sixth grade. By the time Katherine was ten years old, she was ready for high school.

Katherine attended the West Virginia Collegiate Institute. This school grew from a high school and trade school to one of the leading African-American universities.

At the time, West Virginia was still **segregated**. So, Katherine could not attend school with white students. But Katherine's town did not have a high school for African-American students.

Katherine's parents wouldn't let this limit their children's education. So, Katherine and her **siblings** went to an African-American high school in Institute, West Virginia, 125 miles (201 km) away. Katherine's mother lived in Institute with the kids during the school year.

3

MENTORED TOWARD MATHEMATICS

In 1928, Katherine entered high school. She continued to do well in mathematics. Her **geometry** teacher was especially encouraging. And the school principal often pointed out stars and constellations in the sky. This sparked Katherine's interest in astronomy.

Katherine's high school was connected to West Virginia State College. This was an African-American school. When Katherine graduated from high school, she was offered a full **scholarship** to attend the college. Katherine began college in 1933. Her main interests were French, English, and math. She ended up focusing on French and math.

One of Katherine's **mentors** was William Waldron Schieffelin Claytor. He was the third African American in the country to earn a **PhD** in mathematics. Claytor

Katherine learned many life lessons from her father. He valued education and equality and told his children, "You are as good as anybody in this town, but you're no better."

thought she would be a good research mathematician. To help Katherine prepare for such a career, he taught her an advanced form of **geometry**. He knew she would need it in the future.

Katherine graduated in 1937. She received a **bachelor's degree** in both mathematics and French. At 18 years old, she had finished college when most students her age were just beginning!

4

TEACHER, STUDENT, MOTHER

After college, Coleman became a teacher. At the time, this was one of the only professions women could pursue. Coleman's first teaching job was in Marion, Virginia. In Marion, Coleman met and fell in love with James Francis Goble. By 1939, she married James and took his last name.

In 1940, Goble was invited to continue her education at West Virginia University. Although **segregation** was still legal, the school had decided to admit African Americans. She and two others would be the first black students to

SEPARATE IS NOT EQUAL

The US Supreme Court ruled against school segregation in 1954. The ruling marked the beginning of the American **civil rights movement**. This period of mass protest against racial **discrimination** lasted into the 1960s.

attend the school. That summer, Goble entered West Virginia University to study mathematics.

Goble never completed her studies there. She left the school when she had her first daughter. The Gobles later had two more daughters. Goble had set aside her ambition to be a research mathematician. But in 1952, a family member told her about an opportunity that would change her life.

School desegregation was a long process. There were many protests in the 1950s and 1960s. For their safety, some African-American students were escorted to class by bodyguards.

5

WEST END COMPUTER

The National Advisory Committee for **Aeronautics** (NACA) was a federal **agency** for aircraft and flight research. In the 1930s, NACA began to hire white women to work as human computers. And in the 1940s, NACA began hiring African-American women to do the same work.

This new opportunity sounded exciting to Goble. So in 1952, she and her family moved to Newport News, Virginia. There, Goble could pursue a job at NACA. In the meantime, she worked as a substitute math teacher. Later that year, she was approved to work in NACA's Langley

SEGREGATION AT LANGLEY

Until 1958, NACA was **segregated**. The all-black West Computers worked separately from their white peers. They also had to use separate bathrooms and dining facilities. This ended when NACA became part of the National Aeronautics and Space Administration (NASA), which banned segregation.

Goble described her coworkers at Langley as "computers who wore skirts." They could process data efficiently and accurately.

Research Center. She could finally become the research mathematician she had hoped she would be.

Goble's job at NACA's West Area Computing Unit started in June 1953. This unit of about 20 women was known as the West Area Computers. At the time, computing machines were still being developed. They weren't yet able to handle the amount of calculating work that needed to be done. So, people did the calculations by hand. These workers were called computers. The computers at NACA processed data and performed calculations for NACA's research **engineers**.

6

THE FLIGHT RESEARCH DIVISION

Goble only worked with the West Area Computers for about two weeks. She was then transferred to NACA's Flight Research Division. She was told she would temporarily assist in calculations for flight research **engineers**. However, Goble's knowledge of advanced mathematics eventually earned her a permanent position on the team.

Goble spent the next several years contributing to airplane research. Her job was to study data from flight tests and investigate **aeronautic** issues. This process helped flight researchers understand causes of plane crashes and establish new flight regulations.

At NACA, Goble didn't want to only do calculations. She wanted to know why she was doing them. At the time, women did not attend important meetings at NACA.

Goble (*right*) was highly valued by her colleagues throughout her career. They admired her math skills, confidence, and curiosity.

They often didn't know how their work was being applied. But Goble wanted to know, and she became known for asking many questions.

After Goble completed her third year at NACA, she suffered a great personal loss. The year before, doctors had discovered a **tumor** on her husband's brain. Sadly, the tumor couldn't be removed. James Goble died in December 1956.

FROM NACA TO NASA

Goble was greatly saddened by her husband's death, but she remained focused on her work. In October 1957, the Soviet Union launched *Sputnik*, the world's first artificial **satellite**. This marked the beginning of the space race between the United States and the Soviet Union. A Space Task Group was formed to help bring the United States into space. Goble and the flight research **engineers** were part of this task group.

In 1958, NACA became part of the newly formed National **Aeronautics** and Space Administration (NASA). Goble and her team were tasked with writing NASA's first textbook on space travel. They created the first **equations** that would track flight through space.

Now more than ever, Goble wanted to know what happened in NASA meetings. Engineers were presenting new and interesting research, and Goble wanted a front row seat. Finally, she asked the **engineers** if there was a law against her attending. There wasn't, so Goble was finally allowed to join the highly secretive NASA meetings.

As life at work became more exciting, Goble was preparing to marry again. She had met James A. Johnson in the choir at her church. The two married in 1959, and Goble changed her name once more.

There is a model of *Sputnik* at the National Museum of the United States Air Force in Dayton, Ohio.

8

THE GREAT SPACE RACE

At NASA, the space race was well underway. Johnson's knowledge of **geometry** made her very helpful to the Flight Research Division. She cowrote a report on launching, tracking, and returning a spacecraft to a specific location. The report was published in 1960. Johnson was the first woman in the division to receive author credit for a research report.

Johnson's calculations were put to use in 1961. That year, NASA sent the first American into space. Astronaut Alan Shepard launched on May 5. Johnson was responsible for calculating the **trajectory** of Shepard's flight.

For Johnson, this task came down to basic geometry. The flight path took the shape

DID YOU KNOW?

Shepard's flight covered 300 land miles (483 km) but lasted only 15 minutes!

Alan Shepard was one of NASA's first seven astronauts. He
worked for NASA from 1959 to 1974.

John Glenn flew in his last mission when was 77 years old. He was the oldest person to fly in space!

of a parabola, or curve. Johnson was told where on Earth Shepard needed to land. From there, she worked backward to determine when the spacecraft should launch.

In 1962, Johnson faced a greater challenge. NASA was sending astronaut John Glenn into space. But unlike Shepard's flight in 1961, Glenn's spacecraft would orbit Earth. An orbital flight path was harder to calculate than a curved flight path. It had to account for Earth's gravity, shape, and rotation speed.

By this time, NASA was using electronic computers to do these calculations. However, Glenn did not fully trust the calculations of an electronic computer. He knew that Johnson was known for getting the correct answers. He wanted her to make sure the computer calculations were correct.

It took Johnson a day and a half to check that the computer calculations were correct. On February 20, 1962, Glenn became the first American to orbit Earth. He circled the planet three times in five hours!

9

TO THE MOON AND BACK

Johnson's proudest moment in her NASA career came in 1969. Eight years earlier, President John F. Kennedy had announced his goal to put a human on the moon. He had challenged NASA to accomplish this by the end of the 1960s. By 1969, NASA was ready to meet Kennedy's goal with its Apollo 11 **lunar** landing mission.

Johnson had been preparing for Apollo 11 for several years. She wrote reports on lunar orbits and how to navigate in case of electronic failure. She had also calculated **trajectories** for the Lunar Orbiter missions. These were a series of five spacecraft that mapped the surface of the moon. The Lunar Orbiter missions helped NASA decide exactly where Apollo 11 would land.

Now Johnson faced her most demanding task yet. She had to calculate the flight path Apollo 11 would take to and from the moon. First, Apollo 11 would launch into Earth's orbit. From there, it would go into lunar orbit. Finally,

Johnson's job was often stressful, but she loved it. She said, "I went to work every day for 33 years happy. Never did I get up and say, 'I don't want to go to work.'"

a landing unit called the *Eagle* would separate from the main spacecraft, *Columbia*. The *Eagle* would take two astronauts to the surface of the moon.

Apollo 11 launched on July 16, 1969. Four days later, the *Eagle* landed on the moon. Inside it were astronauts Neil Armstrong and Edwin "Buzz" Aldrin. They became the first humans to walk on the moon.

Back on Earth, Johnson followed Apollo 11's progress. Her calculations had put astronauts on the moon! But the biggest challenge was still to come. After 21 hours on the moon, the *Eagle* launched back into **lunar** orbit. To get home, it had to reconnect with the orbit of *Columbia*.

From Earth, Johnson held her breath. If her calculations had been off, the *Eagle* would miss its ride back to Earth. Armstrong and Aldrin would be stranded in space.

Johnson and thousands of other NASA workers watched as their years of hard work produced a successful mission. The *Eagle* successfully connected with *Columbia*.

COLUMBIA AND THE EAGLE

On the moon, Armstrong and Aldrin took photographs and gathered surface samples. Meanwhile, the spacecraft *Columbia* waited in lunar orbit. *Columbia* was on its twenty-seventh orbit when the *Eagle* reconnected with it.

Three days later, Apollo 11 splashed down in the Pacific Ocean, with the astronauts safely aboard. Katherine could finally breathe with relief. Then, she got back to work. There were six more Apollo missions to go.

When he first took a step onto the moon, Neil Armstrong said, "That's one small step for a man, one giant leap for mankind."

10

FUELING THE FUTURE OF SPACE TRAVEL

After the moon landing, Johnson continued to support NASA's remaining Apollo missions. She also helped develop the US Space Shuttle Program, which had its first launch in 1981. Johnson retired from NASA in 1986. Her accomplishments earned her many invitations to speak at conferences and schools. Her speeches inspired many students to pursue careers in Science, **Technology**, **Engineering**, and Mathematics (STEM).

Now in her nineties, Johnson continues to be celebrated for her pioneering work in space travel. In 2015, she received the Presidential Medal of Freedom, the United States' highest non-military honor. In 2016, NASA honored Johnson with the opening of its Katherine G. Johnson Computational Research Facility.

The Presidential Medal of Freedom is just one award Johnson earned in her life. She also received honorary degrees from various universities and several NASA achievement awards!

Countless other honors and awards have recognized Johnson for leading the United States into the Space Age. Her calculations guided Americans among the stars and onto the moon. They continue to pave the way for all future space travel. But even as Johnson made history, she remained humble. To her, she was just doing her job. And for 33 years, she loved every minute of it.

TIMELINE

1918

Katherine Coleman is born on August 26 in White Sulphur Springs, West Virginia.

1937

At 18 years old, Katherine graduates from college with a degree in mathematics and French.

1940

Goble is one of the first black students to desegregate West Virginia University.

1953

Goble joins the West Computing Unit at NACA's Langley Research Center.

1957

The Soviet Union launches *Sputnik.* This kicks off the space race between the United States and Soviet Union.

1958

Goble works on space flight calculations for the newly formed National Aeronautics and Space Administration (NASA).

1961

Johnson calculates the trajectory for astronaut Alan Shepard's space flight.

1962

Johnson checks the electronic computer calculations for astronaut John Glenn's Earth orbit.

1969

Apollo 11 launches on July 16. Johnson's calculations guide the mission to the moon and back.

1986

Johnson retires after 33 years at NASA.

GLOSSARY

aeronautics (air-uh-NAW-tiks)—a science dealing with the design, manufacture, and operation of aircraft.

agency—a part of a government that manages projects in a certain area.

bachelor's degree—a degree that is earned at a college or university, usually after four years of study.

barrier—something that blocks the way or makes something difficult.

civil rights movement—a movement in the United States in the 1950s and 1960s. It consisted of organized efforts to end laws that involved unequal treatment of African Americans.

discrimination (dihs-krih-muh-NAY-shuhn)—unfair treatment, often based on race, religion, or gender.

engineering—the application of science and mathematics to design and create useful structures, products, or systems. A person who does this is an engineer.

equation—a mathematical statement showing equality between two elements, often using an equal sign. A statement such as 1+1=2 is an equation.

geometry—a branch of mathematics that deals with lines, angles, surfaces, and solids.

lunar—of or relating to the moon.

mentor—a trusted adviser or guide.

PhD—doctor of philosophy. Usually, this is the highest degree a student can earn in a subject.

satellite—a manufactured object that orbits Earth. It relays scientific information back to Earth.

scholarship—money or aid given to help a student continue his or her studies.

segregate—to separate an individual or a group from a larger group, especially by race. An act or system of segregating is segregation.

sibling—a brother or a sister.

technology—the use of science in solving problems.

trajectory—the path along which something moves through the air.

tumor—an abnormal mass of cells in the body.

ONLINE RESOURCES

Booklinks
NONFICTION NETWORK
FREE! ONLINE NONFICTION RESOURCES

To learn more about Katherine Johnson, visit **abdobooklinks.com**. These links are routinely monitored and updated to provide the most current information available.

INDEX